My friend Jonah

My friend Jonah

and other dogs I've loved

HERBERT W. CHILSTROM

Illustrations by Gene Basset

HPA | HUFF PUBLISHING ASSOCIATES

Publishing consultant: Huff Publishing Associates, LLC
www.huffpublishing.com
Illustrations by Gene Basset
Cover and interior design by Dorie McClelland, www.springbookdesign.com

Printed in the United States of America
ISBN: 978-0-9895277-6-7
Library of Congress Control Number: 2014948279

Dedicated to Dr. Joel Torstenson, professor of sociology at Augsburg College, Minneapolis, 1947–1977. Joel ushered this small-town Minnesota boy out of my zones of comfort and opened my eyes to a world of need. All of the income from the sale of this book will go toward naming a space to honor Joel in the new Center for Science, Business, and Religion at Augsburg College.

Herb Chilstrom

Contents

Foreword

U.S. Senator Amy Klobuchar

Groucho Marx once quipped: "Outside of a dog, a book is a man's best friend. Inside of a dog it's too dark to read." In *My Friend Jonah—and Other Dogs I've Loved*, retired Lutheran bishop and fellow Minnesotan Herb Chilstrom has written a lovely, moving memoir about his dogs—and, always the preacher, about the lessons to be unleashed (pardon the pun) from looking inside the companionship he shared with Jonah and his four other now-departed friends.

I first got to know Herb Chilstrom through my dad, Jim Klobuchar, and through Bishop Chilstrom's groundbreaking work for the Evangelical Lutheran Church in America. A native of Litchfield, Minnesota, and a graduate of Augsburg College, Herb Chilstrom is—like the protestant church he so ably served—an institution in the state of Minnesota. Having been a pastor to Lutheran congregations in Pelican Rapids, Elizabeth, and St. Peter, Minnesota, and a respected theologian for more than half a century, Bishop Chilstrom has been accompanied on his path by his beloved pets, most recently by his cairn terrier Jonah (no relation to the Old Testament prophet Jonah who, traveling without a dog, spent three days inside a big whale). Dogs are playful, ever-inquisitive creatures that enrich people's daily lives, so it's only fitting that a theologian like Bishop Chilstrom should spend a little time pondering the mysterious wonders of man's best friend.

Whenever I take a walk in my neighborhood or do a summer parade, I am constantly reminded of the special relationship that people have with their dogs. They walk them, they pet them, and they sometimes even dress them up in patriotic garb like red-white-and-blue bandanas and sweaters for the Fourth of July. But most of all, they love them. And like Bishop Chilstrom's love for his flock, the bishop's love for his dogs is palpable in *My Friend Jonah*. With its lively and entertaining writing, a reader could not ask for a better companion as Bishop Chilstrom walks us along his very personal journey—what might be thought of as his dog path of life.

As Bishop Chilstrom, with his master's voice, shepherds us through the lessons his dogs have taught him, from loyalty, discipline, and companionship to forgiveness, curiosity, and rest, he makes us think about the big issues in life: how to live, how to treat others, and even how to die.

My Friend Jonah also brought back vivid memories of my own dog Molly, the spirited, soft-coated wheaten terrier my mom, Rose, brought home in the 1970s who just wouldn't be trained and whose boundless energy was not, under any circumstances, to be contained. This was, remember, decades before the Dog Whisperer.

Molly was my mom's choice from the very beginning. She lobbied for two years to add a little dog to the household, both because it would be a delight for my sister and me, and because she loved what little she knew about Irish terriers. My father enjoyed dogs himself, of course, but it was my mother's ardor that brought Molly into our suburban house. My dad once asked her, why "Molly"? Well, my mom replied, the name somehow suggests sociability. The name Molly, she said, was an invitation to friendship and trust (with a lot of room left for pure fun). And not surprisingly, that's exactly what

Molly became in our household: constantly yelping to be part of the action, even appearing to pout because we wouldn't let her drive the car.

Like most dogs, Molly was loyal and constantly agitating to be part of every family adventure, whether it was a walk in the park, a camping trip, or a game of softball in the backyard. My mom, a big baseball fan, once even insisted that Molly would have made an excellent Minnesota Twins shortstop because she was quick to pounce on the ball. My dad, a longtime sportswriter and columnist for the *Star Tribune*, scored no points with my mom when he pointed out it might have been a long throw to first base for an Irish terrier. Once or twice a year, my dad would actually write a newspaper column about Molly's world and her daily life. Readers responded enthusiastically. When Molly died, it brought tears to our eyes—and the tears reappeared again when we read a letter from a young woman in southwestern Minnesota who wrote to say she'd been so taken by Molly's escapades that she'd read about in my dad's columns that she and her husband named their own infant daughter "Molly."

I read about a study the other day that found dog owners have a lower risk for heart disease. If *My Friend Jonah* is any indication of Bishop Chilstrom's heart, it's a strong one, no doubt strengthened by his lifelong love for dogs. Long live Bishop Chilstrom, and may his fond and thoughtful memories of Jonah and his other dogs inspire new rounds of adoptions at animal shelters everywhere. May Bishop Chilstrom's book also fetch a little joy to anyone who has ever, smiling ear to ear, brought home a brand new puppy or played with a dog in the yard. As the playwright Samuel Gallu wrote in *Give 'Em Hell, Harry*, about President Truman's time in Washington, D.C., "If you want a friend in life, get a dog!"

Prologue

"Look a dog in the eye. Then you will know."

When German pastor, theologian, and author Helmut Thielicke asked an elderly dog lover whether there is a special relationship between dogs and humans, the old fellow replied, "Look a dog in the eye. Then you will know."

This book invites you to "look into the eyes" of five dogs I've known from time to time and loved over a span of seventy years. One I knew for only a few summer weeks, two for a year, and one for nearly fourteen years. But because he was our daily companion for seventeen years after we retired, the major focus of the book is on the one named *Jonah*.

From each of these five dogs I learned some valuable lessons that carried over into my everyday life. At the end of each story is a reflection on those lessons.

The ancestral roots of dogs

Before I share the stories of these five special dogs, let's reflect a bit on how this phenomenal relationship between humans and dogs evolved.

It's commonly agreed among biologists and archaeologists that all dogs have evolved from wolves—*canis lupus*. The gradual move from wolf to dog took tens of thousands of years. It's fair to ask how some wolves became so deeply connected to humans.

When and where did it happen? This is a hotly debated question.

Until recently it was thought that the transition occurred in the Middle East or in southern China. But more recent DNA studies make the case for Western Europe.

Whenever and wherever it happened, the speculation is that some wolves were smarter than others. After following the hunters/gatherers, picking and licking over the scraps that humans left behind, some wolves had a better idea.

Let's have some fun and imagine how all this happened from the perspective of wolves.

"Let's pretend we're not so mean"

We'll begin by turning our calendars all the way back to, let's say, 11,259 BCE. A pack of wolves is having its "annual convention." The moon is full as the chair of the convention, a grizzled old male named Adam, tells them all to stop baying at the moon. He asks if any of the delegates have new ideas on how to improve their lot in life. A young male named Brutus steps forward. (Only males were permitted to attend wolf conventions in these early days.)

"My fellow canis lupians, I have an idea," volunteers Brutus.

"Another impractical, harebrained suggestion," the older wolves murmur in unison.

"Hey, you guys. Listen up. What happens," asks Brutus, "every time we close in on anything those greedy, selfish bipeds kill? They come rushing out of their caves throwing sticks and stones at us. How many of you elders are blind in one eye and walk with a limp because of those fierce attacks? So here's my plan. Let's just lie down a stone's throw or two from them, making like we're benign and harmless. We'll wait until after dark before we go for those last bits and pieces."

His suggestion brings only bays and howls. "We've never done it that way before," the old wolves agree. "It'll never work. Forget it."

But the next day Brutus and his friend Rolf are hunting together and come upon a group of bipeds who have just gorged themselves sick on a succulent wild boar.

"Okay, Rolf, here's a chance to try my new idea," suggests Brutus. So he and Rolf sit down in plain sight of the hunters and feign harmlessness. No snarling or snapping. They make no move to come closer to the carcass. After the hunters go into their cave for an early evening nap, Brutus and Rolf creep quietly forward and fill their bellies. The bipeds sleep through it all.

As darkness settles over the forest the hunters drag themselves out and settle in for a late night gabfest around the campfire. One of them says, "Hey, did you guys notice those wolves? They must be sick! Or could it be that there are a few wolves who aren't as bad as the rest?"

And so began a small change in attitude toward some wolves.

"They're as slow as toads"

Now fast forward to, let's say, 10,652 BCE. By this time the wolves, like humans, are divided into two denominations—the Traditional and the Reformed. The smarter ones—the Reformed—are at their annual convention. (There are still no females allowed.) But now another young wolf by the name of Rudy has a notion.

"I've got a great idea," says Rudy. "Bipeds don't seem to mind when we hang around their camp. They think our pups are really cute. But we still get nothing but scraps after a hunt. So let's try something new. You all see how slow they are, trying to run on two legs when four would be more efficient. Next time they go out on a hunt, let's follow them by two stones' throws. When we see a rabbit, we'll race by them, run down the rabbit, and leave it on the ground for them to pick up."

Once more the majority howls and hoots at the idea. "We've never done it that way before. It'll never work," they all growl.

The next morning Rudy and his friend Max sneak out of the pack and follow the hunters.

As soon as the bipeds flush a rabbit, Rudy and Max dash by them like streaks of lightning and bring the rabbit down in a flash. The hunters think they've lost their prey.

But to their amazement, the wolves leave it there. In an hour they down three more.

Around the fire that night the hunters lick their chops and devour the tasty meat from the fat succulent rabbits. Then one of them speaks up, "Hey, you guys. Did you see what those wolves did for us today? Amazing! Don't you think they deserve something for their good work?"

And so begins the eons of man feeding wolf. No more sticks in the eye or stones in the groin. Man is becoming the servant of the wolf. And wolf is beginning to become—you guessed it—a dog.

"They can't hear a thing"

Now let's move on to, let's say, 8,479 BCE. Another convention of the Reformed branch is in session. (There are still no she-wolves allowed at the meeting.)

"Any new ideas?" asks Willie, the old chairman of the pack. "Yes," speaks up Oliver, a younger wolf/dog. "With ears pinned flat to the sides of their heads, how can those odd-looking, clumsy creatures hear anything at all? We've got eighteen muscles in our ears. How many do they have? Only six! Our ears are like big cups. We can point them in any direction. Some day one of their smart descendants will discover that we can pick up forty-five thousand units of frequency. And they? Only twenty-three thousand. Our hearing is almost twice as sharp as theirs.

"So let's just doze lightly through the night. But the minute we hear something suspicious out in the dark, let's bellow out a loud howl. When those humans see that we saved yesterday's quarry, our breakfast will be bigger and better than ever!"

But even the Reformed wolves think it's a silly idea. "We've never done it that way before. It'll never work."

But that very night Oliver hears some noises in the dark woods. He can't contain himself. Near the mouth of the cave he lets out a blood-curdling yelp that rouses the bipeds from their deep slumber and brings them running out of their beds just as a she-bear is about to make off with their breakfast.

Next morning not only Oliver, but the whole pack gets an extra helping of savory meat.

"They can't smell a thing"

By 6,685 BCE, let's say, the Reformed wolves are beginning to allow females in the pack to have voice (but not vote, of course!) at the annual convention.

It was there that Lucy says she has an idea. The males howl to high heaven. "A female? You've got an idea? Give us a break!"

"Hey, you guys, listen here," snarls Lucy. "You all know those bipeds can't smell an angry mama grizzly until she has them by the throat. Years from now advanced bipeds will discover what we already know. They have only fifty million olfactory cells in their noses. And how many do we have? Two hundred and twenty million! Our sense of smell is almost five times better than theirs. They'll thank us for saving their skins with an early warning using our keen noses. And, yes, we'll even help them find birds and rats and squirrels and raccoons and all kinds of other creatures they love to eat but can't smell until they stumble over them."

Now humans and wolf/dogs—ancestors of our keenest hunting dogs— were walking side-by-side through field and forest.

Yes, it worked. And guess what? More food!

"They can't see in the dark"

Now we move to, let's say 5,103 BCE. Convention time again and Tilly, a young wolf/dog, has an idea. Now the pack really howls! "A kid your age ought to keep still."

But Tilly says, "I see something every night you elders miss. You doze off too soon. I notice that every night when those sleepy bipeds go out of the cave for their final visit to the woods they stub their toes on rocks and logs and yelp when they get a twig poked into their eyes. Do we have that problem? Not at all. They may have better vision in the daylight. But come dark and the advantage is ours. So let's go a few steps ahead of them on their nighttime outings. When we jump a log they'll know they better slow up a bit and be more careful."

It worked. Tilly was right. Now dog and master were fully bonded, both day and night.

And, yes, more food!

All in the family

So it was that wolves became dogs, and dogs and humans became family. It was a mutual benefit society.

Tell me, fellow dog lovers—does all this sound a bit familiar? I've seen it myself, and so have you. You love and care for your dog; your dog loves and cares for you. With each of my dogs, the pattern has been the same. All of these wolf-descended canines conditioned me into becoming a total servant of their needs.

Each one mastered his master. I loved it. And so do you.

Now let me tell you about my five dogs I've loved, beginning with Duke, a collie; then Chief, a Chesapeake Bay/Labrador retriever mix; and then a succession of three cairn terriers—Toto, Obie, and Jonah.

Duke, that stately, elegant collie

Collies—favorites for a good reason

The first dog I fell in love with was Duke, a magnificent collie.

Just how he and all collie dogs descended from wolves is hidden in the mysteries of evolution. As we know them today, this breed originated in northern England and Scotland. Because they seemed to have a natural instinct for herding, they were useful to shepherds in that rocky and rugged landscape. Sometime in the nineteenth century, thanks in large part to the interest of Queen Victoria, collies emerged as popular pets for families.

A robust collie can weigh up to seventy pounds and live as long as fifteen to sixteen years. When well trained, they are almost always good natured and easy to manage. For that reason, they make good companions for every member of the family, from toddlers to grandpas and grandmas. But, like all dogs, they require care and attention. Because their long coats can easily pick up burrs and small, thorny sticks, collies need daily brushing. And any attention to their needs is rewarded by a happy, content dog.

No room in this house

Any hope that I would ever have a dog like this was out of the question. We were a poor family living on the edge of Litchfield, Minnesota, my hometown. After leaving the farm in 1935 my parents moved into a small, two-bedroom house with no running water or bathroom. Lots of our neighbors shared our lot in life in those years of the Great Depression.

Like many others, my father, Wally, had minimum-wage jobs much of the time in the late 1930s, including some Works Progress Administration (WPA) projects. After World War II broke out he got a job at a local, powdered-milk plant, once more at minimum salary.

My mother, Ruth, was primarily a homemaker who not only cared for her family in the house and kitchen, but was also the primary caretaker of a huge vegetable garden and a flock of laying hens on our large corner lot. The produce, eggs, and meat filled the larder in the summer and fall and carried us through much of the winter. Every week she baked huge loaves of tasty rye bread, the staple of our diet. To make ends meet Wally and Ruth also did the custodial work at our local Lutheran church. Every member of the family pitched in to dust pews, mow grass, and sweep floors.

Having a dog, however, was out of the question. Not only was there "no room at the inn"; there simply was no money to buy dog food. And, given the size of our family—eight hungry kids—there were no leftovers for a hungry canine.

An unexpected opportunity

Then one day in the summer of my eleventh year all that changed. Our family physician Dr. Cecil, his wife, Isabel, and son, Tom, lived across town in a nice neighborhood full of lovely homes and tree-shaded streets.

The doctor's family had a dog named Duke, a tall-standing collie with a gold-hued face and magnificent white vest. I was certain this dog was the finest canine in our town of four thousand.

I had already fallen in love with collie dogs. Margaret Shmid, our red-headed sixth-grade teacher, shared daily excerpts from *Lassie Come Home* with us. After lunch my classmates and I would sit dreamily caught up in the adventurous world of imagination as we followed the fortunes and misfortunes of Lassie. We fought back tears as we thought of her banishment to a far-off corner of Great Britain. We sat in rapt attention as Lassie found her way, treacherous mile after treacherous mile, over the craggy English hills and through briar patches, until she arrived back at her beloved home and family.

Back in the real world of 1943, our country was in the throes of World War II. Dr. Cecil was called to military duty. In that summer Isabel and young Tom were able to spend several weeks with him on a military base.

Wonder of wonders, they asked me to take care of Duke! I couldn't have been more proud and delighted. To think that they chose me and trusted me—it was unbelievable.

Now I would have my very own "Lassie," if only for a few sunny weeks of summer. I need not worry about money for dog food because Dr. Cecil would give me money to buy all the huge bags of delicious dog food this big collie demanded.

A memorable summer

Duke was a magnificent creature, large and strong and friendly. He loved to play fetch. Even though my skin-and-bones body didn't weigh much more than his, I wrestled with him in the front yard for hours as my mother looked on with delight from the window next to her sewing machine. With

his strong chain leash always firmly in hand, my younger brother Dave and I took Duke on long walks around town and out into the countryside. I'm sure almost everyone in our town knew a poor kid like me couldn't possibly afford to have a magnificent, purebred dog like Duke. I felt like the luckiest kid in Litchfield.

After some weeks I began to imagine that Duke was all mine. The bond was so deep that I couldn't believe he would ever want to return to the doctor's family.

A first taste of grief

Then the inevitable happened. Near the end of summer word came that Dr. Cecil would be home on furlough, and his wife and son would return with him in time for the start of the school year.

On the appointed day I walked slowly and sadly from our home in one corner of town to the doctor's home in the other, savoring every minute I could stretch out on that last trek with Duke. With every block I felt lonelier. I kept wondering against all reason: Could it be that Duke is so attached to me that he's maybe forgotten the doctor and his family?

The painful answer came when we reached the corner a block from the doctor's home. At that moment Dr. Cecil happened to step out the back door. Seeing Duke, he called for him. The big collie made one strong lunge, ripping the chain leash from my hand and dashing like a gazelle across the grassy lawns to his waiting master.

Though he had received only the very best and loving care from me, Duke, like Lassie, had come home.

It was as though every last shred of hope had been yanked out of my heart. I felt sad to the core of my being. No, Duke had not forgotten where he had been since he was a puppy. No, he wasn't my dog after all.

A long walk home

I don't recall what Dr. Cecil said to me. I'm sure he patted me on the back and thanked me for caring for Duke. He probably even gave me a nice tip for doing such a good job. It didn't matter. I was in no state of mind to hear anything he said or appreciate anything he gave me.

As I walked away I wanted to cry. But eleven-year-old boys don't cry. Crestfallen and despondent, I retreated slowly, block after block, down the streets and past the shops on Main Street, choking back tears and feeling like a boy who had been abandoned by his closest friend.

Back home, I covered my sadness. I'm sure my family had no idea how heavy my heart felt in those next weeks.

It was my first real taste of grief—the price we pay for love.

It wouldn't be the last.

What I learned from Duke
Loyalty

As I reflect on my time with Duke I realize it made no sense that Duke should have abandoned the attachment he had for Dr. Cecil and his family. That was where he belonged. I could give him love and affection for a short time, but not for the long haul.

And so it is with life. As the years unfold we develop relationships of many kinds. Some are very brief and casual. Others may be long-term, but are never more than superficial. Still others are intense for a short time, but then cool over the years. But some are deep and intense and last for a lifetime. For most of us, there are a few friends, maybe only two or three, to whom we are loyal until we die. Within our closest circles—parents, siblings, and bonded friends—the loyalty is usually very intense. These are the people we would die for if necessary at a moment's notice. To them we will always be loyal.

Yes, Duke taught me about loyalty.

"I think we should call him Chief"

What good is a gun without a dog?

After I was ordained in 1958 Corinne and I went to serve a small two-point parish at Elizabeth and Pelican Rapids, Minnesota. We lived in a tiny apartment while the new parsonage was being built. Once we moved into our nicely decorated home I began to think about getting a dog. This was hunting country. One thousand of Minnesota's more than ten thousand lakes are located in Otter Tail County where we lived. Waterfowl ponds were everywhere. Not far off were the open plains of the Red River Valley where pheasants and grouse were abundant. This was a hunter's paradise.

By coincidence Edwin, a cattle trucker, said he thought Pastor Chilstrom should do some hunting. He was not a man of field and pond himself but had won a sixteen-gauge Winchester shotgun in a contest. We agreed on a price of twenty-five dollars, a bargain for a fine firearm like that.

But what is a gun without a dog? Ever so gently I broached the subject with Corinne. I played to her sensitive side, mentioning that as a boy our family could not afford a gun for hunting, and I could only tag along as my pals took delight in shooting pheasants, ducks, and rabbits. And, of course, I underscored my love for Duke, that wonderful collie, and my longing that one day I might have a dog of my very own.

She was understandably reluctant. The new parsonage hardly seemed a good place to accommodate a canine. What would the members of the congregation think? I dropped the subject, but hung on to my dream.

A little help from Karla

In the summer of 1960 three-year-old niece Karla and her two-year-old sister Tami came to stay with us for a couple of weeks while their parents awaited the arrival of baby brother Jeffrey.

One day I saw an ad in the local weekly newspaper announcing that a family in the country had a litter of mixed Labrador/Chesapeake pups, free to anyone who would give one a good home. I mentioned it to Karla. My strategy worked. She lit up with delight at the mention of a puppy. How could Corinne withstand the pressure of a three-year-old toddler and her uncle?

I put a cardboard box in the back seat of our 1960 Chevy Biscayne. Karla and I headed for the county.

Let's call him Chief

Karla and I watched as several little, furry brown balls tumbled over the grass. "That one," squealed Karla as she pointed to the puppy that ran toward us. She thought this one was just right for Uncle Herb.

On our way back to town I asked Karla what name she thought we should give to our new puppy. With little hesitation she erupted, "I think we should call him *Chief*." Why Chief? Where did that come from? I had no idea. But Chief it was.

An ideal mix

The mixture of Labrador and Chesapeake seemed ideal to me. As the name implies, Labradors originated on the east coast of Canada in the province by that name. The dog was originally known as the "St. John's Water Dog." When traders from England visited in the early eighteenth century they noted the dog's extraordinary skill at hunting and retrieving along and in coastal waters. They brought some of the dogs to England and, as we say, the rest is history. Today's variety of basic colors—black, yellow, and chocolate— all originate from those early labs.

In time it became apparent that Labradors were also fine family dogs, gentle with children and easily trained to be guides to the blind. Yes, and with their keen noses, law officers eventually chose this breed to aid in their work.

Indeed, having even a half-Labrador was a good choice.

Chesapeakes or Chesapeake Bay dogs also are named after their place of origin, the east coast of the United States. These dogs too came into prominence in the early and middle nineteenth century. While male labs can range up to sixty-five to seventy pounds in weight, Chesapeake dogs are a bit smaller and more agile, somewhat better suited for woods and thick underbrush. If a lab is more at home in the water than on land, the Chesapeake is more at home on land than in the water. But both dogs, when well trained, are effective in either environment.

How could I be so fortunate?

Boundaries that didn't hold

Several months after Chief joined our family, six-week-old Mary arrived at our home, our first child. The bond was strong. Chief, still a pup himself, clearly loved this other new "pup."

Our firm rule was that Chief must be primarily an outside dog with access to no more than the kitchen with its linoleum floor where "accidents" during training time could easily be taken care of. When we sat in the living room Chief would spread his paws right up to the edge of the carpet and look longingly at us. "Hey," he seemed to say with his pleading eyes, "I thought I was going to be a member of this family. Why are you leaving me out of all the fun?"

We held to the boundary rule until he simply could not resist placing his brown paws a few inches on to the soft carpet toward Mary and me. Finally, the urge was simply too overpowering. On all fours he slithered over and rolled against us. Our resistance melted. Now he rollicked with us. Dog, dad, and little girl were fully bonded.

"Don't fence me in"

I built a sturdy doghouse out of scraps of leftover lumber from the parsonage building project. On my slim, first parish salary we could scarcely afford dog food. There were no extra funds for a backyard fence. That meant tying Chief to the doghouse when we were away. It didn't work. He barked, of course, to the dismay of the neighbors. Within months he quickly grew into a strong, restless dog, eager to explore the world. He pulled and jerked until the chain broke and he was free to roam.

It wasn't long until he was in the yard of the widow next door. For reasons I never understood, Chief seemed to have taste buds that craved dahlia bulbs, especially the prized ones. Soon her tubers were in his tummy.

Facing hard reality

The two congregations I served were both "on life support." With only a handful of members at each place I had no choice but to be out calling morning, noon, and evening to try to build up their numbers.

I also was beginning to get involved in activities that took me out of town on occasion for speaking engagements and board responsibilities.

It all meant that I had little time to train Chief for hunting and even less to get to cornfields and duck ponds to use him and my gun. It wasn't fair to deprive this wonderful friend of the life he had been born to live. This dog was not meant for town living. He belonged in the country where he could roam freely and be trained to hunt.

Ever so reluctantly I faced reality.

Good-bye my dear Chief

Shortly after Chief's first birthday and not long before we left on our summer vacation, I put an ad in the local newspaper with no price attached. Soon a farmer was at the door with his pickup truck. Off went Chief and the doghouse, both for five dollars.

I retreated to my study, thinking I would just work on my sermon for the next Sunday. I would try to forget Chief.

I should have known better. In moments my head was on my desk, and I was sobbing like a little boy. And that's who I was, once more—a little boy who couldn't have a dog.

Once more I was learning that the price we pay for love is a wrenching pain deep in our hearts.

What I learned from Chief
Discipline

Dogs that are meant to be house pets may need little training. A few sessions at dog school may do the trick.

But hunting dogs, even those who also become house pets, require hours and hours of patient training over many months, with reinforcement through their entire lives. It's the investment a hunting dog owner must spend if his dog is to become a companion in field, woods, and pond. There are no shortcuts.

Furthermore, one soon learns that some hunting dogs take naturally to the training sessions, some require much more time and effort, and some, even if they come with the finest pedigree, simply will not hunt. But one never knows how a hunting dog will turn out unless one invests ample time and effort to learn all this about one dog.

Isn't that the way it is in our human families? Child rearing takes much time and effort. A father or mother who isn't willing to invest many years in the task of raising a child should think twice before launching into parenthood. Yes, and even when one has spent that effort, one can never be certain of the outcome. We do our best.

But a dog also makes us take a closer look at ourselves. Over time we learn that the best things in life come only after we've been willing to exercise strong discipline and hard work in the venture of daily living. The "treats" of life are only for those who have "done their duty."

Freedom

Chief also taught me that the purpose of discipline and hard work is that we might be free. A couple of examples:

I have boundless admiration for two of my neighbors who are concert pianists. When they sit on stage at two pianos, with fingers flying across the keys, it looks so easy to me, one who has never had a single lesson. But then I walk by their home and listen as they work those keys hour after hour, going over the same scores again and again to make certain they are correct and that their music is perfectly coordinated.

My own profession is another good example. After a sermon it's common for folks to come up to their pastor, priest, or rabbi and say, "That was a wonderful message. It looks so easy for you to preach, so effortless for you to give an address." They have no idea how many hours one invests in a well-prepared and effectively-delivered speech, how many starts and stops in the course of the writing, how many times a phrase or sentence or paragraph has been rewritten.

And so it is with all of life. The rewards of freedom—the joys of accomplishment—are the end result of strict discipline and hard labor. As a friend of mine likes to say, "It takes a lot of hard work to make things look easy."

Thanks, Chief, for the lessons of life you taught me.

Toto—a pet for the whole family

A dog in this place? Not a chance

In 1962 we moved from Minnesota to New Jersey where I assumed a position as professor of religion at a small church college. Our family now included not only Mary, but also Christopher, who arrived in 1962 just prior to our move. In 1966 Andrew, our third child, joined the family. We had our hands full. The thought of having a dog never even crossed my mind. Here we were, living in the heart of the New York City metropolitan area where one New Jersey suburb ran into another. Yes, there were a few dogs in the community. But for us? No, this wasn't even a remote possibility. I was traveling a good deal of the time, preaching here and there up and down the East Coast most every Sunday, and at times being away on teaching assignments in congregations and at conventions. On top of all this, I was pursuing graduate studies at Princeton Seminary one day a week. No, no time for a dog.

Now it was Corinne's turn

One day I was sitting at my desk at the college when the phone rang. It was Corinne. She never called me on campus unless it was something urgent. "Herb," she said with hesitation, "the children and I are at Doreen's home. The kids have been having a wonderful time with her children." That seemed no good reason for her to call me at the office.

Then the unexpected plea: "There's a family next door that has a puppy. It's a cute little cairn terrier. The kids really love this little dog. It's the last one left of the litter, and the family is leaving on a trip tomorrow. Doreen thinks we should adopt this puppy for our kids."

Could this be—Corinne asking *me* if we could have a dog?

Whoa, I thought. Yes, I'd love to have a dog again. But we could never afford to buy one in this expensive area. "How much do they want for it?" I asked. "Well," she said with more hesitation, "seventy-five dollars."

Long pause. On my young professor's meager salary this seemed completely out of the realm of possibility.

Then I asked some dumb questions: "So the kids have seen the dog and played with it, have they?" "Yes," she replied. "And they really love this puppy, do they?" The fact that this "leftover" was the runt of the litter and probably would never weigh more than thirteen to fourteen pounds at most, thus eating only a meager diet, didn't help convince me that we could afford a dog.

But there was little point in delaying the inevitable. I knew the decision had been made. "All right, bring him home," I said. "Somehow we'll manage."

And manage we did. My earlier love for a dog came bounding back the moment I laid eyes on the new puppy. How could one not love a face like this? Just as those smart wolves from which he was descended had become family, so this little terrier was immediately a total member of ours.

A long history in Scotland

Before I get more deeply enmeshed in the story of this little bundle of happiness, and since he was followed in our family by two more cairn terriers, I need to fill in a little background about this breed.

All terriers, of course, get their name from the Latin word *terra*, meaning "earth." Terriers, coming in many varieties, have in common a penchant for "sticking to the ground." They have been bred over the years to search out smaller furry and slithery ground creatures for their hunting masters as well as for their own diet.

Cairn terriers originated in Scotland and, specifically, from the island of Skye. The familiar Skye terriers are well known and loved around the world. With their fox-like ears and somewhat elongated bodies, they make good hunters as well as excellent pets. Their original utilitarian purpose was to hunt out varmints of all kinds on the stony island where they were bred and developed.

At some later time breeders seemed to want a smaller dog with the same characteristics. Over time the cairn terrier evolved, getting its name from the stone heaps or "cairns" that dot the Scottish countryside. They were bred to dig out rats, mice, rabbits, moles, voles, snakes, and any other small creatures that seek refuge under stone heaps, wood piles, and buildings. One account suggests that in order to develop the strongest dogs possible a breeder would place a cairn terrier in an enclosed space with a wolverine, one of the most vicious wild animals. If the cairn survived, it would be bred. This seems cruel indeed to any modern lover of cairn terriers. But little wonder that their stout bodies are packed with power and vitality.

In the 1800s breeders in western Scotland tended to favor the lighter hue of some cairns. In time a white-coated dog emerged. Those became the forerunners of the West Highland terriers, one of the most popular breeds of any dog today.

In the early 1900s breeders agreed to separate these "cousin" dogs, keeping the lines distinct. Cairn terriers vary in color from black to brindle to grey to light brown. Often the colors are blended.

Let's call him Toto

Now back to our own cairn terrier.

Because we had seen and enjoyed *The Wizard of Oz* with that courageous little cairn terrier named *Toto,* it was easy for our family to agree that this puppy should be our very own "Toto."

We stressed to our children that a large part of our concession to their desire to have a puppy was that the care of Toto would be primarily their responsibility. They readily agreed and seldom complained when it was time to feed and walk him. He was their bedroom companion from the start. He heard many of their prayers, heartaches, and dreams, just as a good dog should.

When we moved to St. Peter, Minnesota, in 1970, Toto, of course, came along as part of our entourage. Corinne drove our 1962 Chevrolet Impala with our three children as passengers. I drove our old beat-up 1957 VW Beetle with plants in the back-seat and Toto as my copilot. The Impala climbed the Allegheny Mountains with ease. I would struggle up the steep grades in the Beetle as they zipped by. On the down slopes Toto and I barreled past them as the children waved and Toto wagged his tail. It was an adventure.

Toto continued to be primarily the responsibility of the children. But as they grew and developed friendships and other interests, Corinne and I did more and more of his care and keeping, especially Corinne. We didn't mind. He was now just as much a friend of ours as he was of the children.

Our little watchdog

When we moved to Edina, Minnesota, in 1976 Toto was again part and parcel of our home and family. One memorable night we were all asleep on the second level. Toto usually slept in Andrew's bedroom. But on that night we heard him barking downstairs on the first level. Corinne, assuming he had been awakened by noise on our busy street, went down to bring him back upstairs. When she got there he was in the kitchen near the back door, barking as fiercely as the original Toto did when he neared the great Wizard. Corinne noticed that the back door was standing slightly ajar. Then she saw that her sewing machine was missing. Indeed we had had a burglar in the house! When the police investigated the incident they determined that our door locks were easy to penetrate. The job I had put off now got done the next day—installation of dead bolts on all outer doors.

Little cairns were never bred to be watch dogs. But Toto saved us from major losses, proving to be our little hero.

Several years later a neighbor up the street was arrested for numerous burglaries, no doubt including the one at our home. He was a former member of a Milwaukee mafia crime ring who had squealed on his cronies. The FBI gave him an assumed name, protective custody, and a lovely home in our neighborhood. We learned that one never knows who's living next door or down the street! But we also came to appreciate the value of a little dog, yes, even the runt of the litter.

By the early 1980s Mary and Chris had left home, and it was Andrew who bonded most closely with Toto. He absorbed a good deal of love and understanding from Andrew, as well as from Corinne and me.

Aging and the inevitable

Toto began to show signs of advanced age in his thirteenth year. One morning he could not go to his dish for a drink of water. It was time. I took him to the vet and had him put to sleep.

My plan was to bury him at our Lake Lida cabin near Pelican Rapids, some four hours from home. On my way to a speaking engagement in Iowa I made a large circle north to the lake. I dug a deep hole near the lakeshore. There I gently placed his body and covered it with soft soil under the warm sod.

I was on a tight schedule and needed to rush off, but not before sitting down on the deck for a few minutes. Once more I was weeping like a little kid. How deep the bonds, how dear these pets, how integral to our family life—it all came together in those moments.

The tears flowed for many miles down the road on my way south to Iowa.

Once again I felt the cost of love. When I wrote our 1982 family Christmas letter a few weeks later I included this paragraph:

> *The saddest day of the year for all five of us was October 4. Our little grey cairn terrier, Toto, had to be put to sleep. That it happened on the eight-hundredth anniversary of the death of St. Francis of Assisi seemed appropriate. Toto was a special friend to all of us these nearly fourteen years. Like the more famous Toto, we think he may be waiting for us someday at the end of the Yellow Brick Road with his wagging tail and friendly bark.*

Now it made no sense to have a dog. Andrew was caught up in school and sport activities. After a career in nursing, Corinne was studying at the seminary to become a Lutheran minister. I was fully engaged in my work as the bishop for many of the Lutherans in Minnesota.

Would I ever again have a dog? Would I ever want to go through the inevitable sorrow of watching a dog die?

What I learned from Toto
Companionship

Do dogs have feelings? When our spirits are down, do they share our sadness? When we feel up, do they sense our elation? When we're sick, do they wonder what's wrong with us? When we treat them badly, do they think it's always their fault? And when we die, do they miss us?

Biologists and researchers can't seem to answer these questions with certainty. Some think a dog's only motivation for pleasing us is to make certain, like those ancient wolves, that they get another meal.

Others are convinced that dogs occupy a higher rung on the ladder of living things and can actually sense our changing human emotions and conditions.

Stories help:

My friend Bill loved Lucy, his white miniature poodle. When cancer took him down and left him bedridden for months, Lucy was his constant bedside companion both day and night. An hour before Bill died Lucy leapt down from the bed, left the room, and never returned. Did Lucy understand that Bill was about to leave this world? You be the judge.

When Randy became fatally ill, Rex, his golden lab, like Bill's Lucy, was at his bedside day and night. When Randy died Rex would go to the first landing and then stop. He would never again go the full flight of stairs to Randy's bedroom. Did Rex have feelings of loss for Randy? You be the judge.

As for our family, there's no question in our minds that Toto played a large part in our daily physical and emotional well-being. Morning and evening walks were good not only for Toto, but for all of us.

It also can be said that a dog relates to various members of the family in different ways. Teenage Andrew, who had developed a special bond with Toto after Mary and Chris were off to college, spent a good deal of time with Toto. Every night Toto settled into his place at the foot of Andrew's bed. After he died and before I took him off to be buried, Andrew went to the basement where Toto's body was kept for a day or two and had quiet time with him.

Who can measure the wholeness Toto brought to all of us as we went for long walks with him, stroked his back, laughed at his antics, and quietly poured out to him our feelings of sadness, joy, confusion, pleasure, and hope?

Yes, Toto was a true companion to all five of us.

Retirement: "Let's call him Obie"

Testing the waters

We had scarcely settled into our retirement home on Lake Lida near Pelican Rapids, Minnesota, in 1995. It was now more than fifteen years since Toto had died. Because we had lived in a condominium in the Chicago area for most of those years and because my work took me away from home almost half of the time, having a dog had been out of the question.

But now that we were settled in the country, I started to think of how ideal it would be to have a canine in our home.

One morning over breakfast I decided to test the waters. "Wouldn't it be fun to have a dog again?" I said to Corinne. Knowing how much she enjoyed Toto, I ventured that our lakeside home and yard would be exactly the right place for another cairn terrier.

Corinne's reaction was one of hesitation and practicality. Yes, we planned to travel. Yes, we would both no doubt be speaking at events here and there. Yes, there was that first trying year of training. Yes, it would tie us down at a time when we wanted to be free to come and go as we pleased.

I reminded her that there was a fine kennel in town where a dog could be boarded. I ventured that a smaller dog like another cairn terrier could easily travel with us on road trips. Then I let the subject rest.

An eye on the pet section

Each day, however, my eye would wander to the pet section of the *Minneapolis Star Tribune.* With our frequent trips to Minneapolis to visit family, picking up a puppy would be no problem.

But cairn terriers seldom appeared in the ads. When they did, I soon discovered that because our edition of the newspaper was a later one the puppies were gone by the time I called. Since I was determined to have another cairn, my hopes grew dim as the weeks rolled by.

Then one day we decided to drive to Fargo to see a movie. I picked up a copy of the *Fargo Forum.* As I scanned the film guide my eye wandered across the page to the pet section. There, to my amazement, was an ad for cairn terrier puppies! I could scarcely believe my eyes. In this more rural area it was uncommon to find much other than the usual run of hunting dogs and mixed-breed mutts.

A cairn in our backyard

I picked up the phone and dialed the 218 area code number in the advertisement. That code covers all of northern Minnesota as far as the Canadian border. These cairn puppies could be anywhere from the Fargo area to Duluth to International Falls.

"Do you have any puppies left?" I asked the woman who answered the phone, expecting the reply would be the same as I had heard from the Twin Cities. "Yes, I have two of them," she replied. "It seems very few folks in this part of the country know much about cairn terriers. I don't get any calls for them."

I scarcely dared ask, "Where do you live?"

"I live just a few miles east of Detroit Lakes," she said.

Could this be, I wondered, only twenty miles up the road?

Which one will it be?

The next morning we were at Evelyn's door bright and early. Her husband Pete brought two adorable cairn puppies to the kitchen. We played with them for a bit and decided on the one that kept coming to us. We wrote out a check, collected the pedigree documents, and were on our way home. Corinne wrapped the fury ball in a warm blanket and showered him with his first loving hugs as we made our happy way home through pristine lakes surrounded by maple and white birch forests that dotted the countryside.

What's in a name?

As we drove and looked into his bright eyes we talked about what we should name this new member of our retirement family. "Well," Corinne said, "the pastor of our church has a dog named *Amos*." We agreed that the very next book among the Minor Prophets in the Old Testament might be an apt one: Obadiah. "Let's call him *Obie*," Corinne said. So Obie it was.

Adjusting to a "type A" puppy

From the moment he hit the floor at our lake home we knew we had an aggressive, superactive canine on our hands. In the next weeks anything loose—a rag, sox, my pajamas, a shoe—anything was fair game for Obie to grasp with his teeth and shake violently. With front paws on one end and his sharp, little incisors on the other, he soon ripped to shreds anything within reach. This little fellow would need firm discipline and patient training. We were determined to "go by the book" and shape him into the best-behaved doggie in Otter Tail County.

In spite of his mischievous behavior, how could we help but love and admire this little bundle of energy? His stiffer brindle outer hair covered an inner layer that was as soft as velvet and almost orange in its hue.

Settling into the family routine

Having learned earlier that the secret to dog training is routine, we ordered our day around his needs for food, rest, exercise, and play. Obie loved our half-mile morning and evening walks through the meadow across the road and up the lane that overlooked the lake. In summer I cut a path through the quarter-mile meadow; in winter I plowed it with my snowblower.

On frigid, sunny, winter days Obie enjoyed stretching out for a nap in front of the sliding doors that faced south to the lake. It was the ideal spot for my afternoon nap, too, as I bonded with my new little friend.

Those genes from ancient days

We learned again why cairns were known as "ground dogs." Obie had no interest whatever in sharing our stunning view of Lake Lida from the highest crest on the lane. No, he only wanted to put his supersensitive nose to the ground and sniff and scratch at every gopher, vole, and badger hole he could find. At times when he was distracted, Corinne would linger with him as I walked ahead a half block or so and hid behind a bush. When I called "Obie! Obie! Obie!" his pointed ears perked up, and he took off like a bullet until he found me.

Demands to be part of the family

Early in his puppyhood we tried to "kennel" him, just as the book suggested. We thought he might like to be in the shop just off the kitchen, nestled quietly into his bed all by himself. We were wrong. He barked and wrestled with the metal door until it relented. He came bounding and barking into our bedroom as if to say, "Hey, you can't do this to me! I thought I was going to be part of this family. Don't you know that dogs like to live in packs?"

We decided then and there that a soft blanket at the foot of our bed was the only place for this little, people-loving extrovert.

We also decided, though cairn terriers do not shed, to keep him off the living room furniture. He obeyed, but very reluctantly. He soon figured out a way to circumvent this dilemma. He climbed to a step on our open stairway overlooking the living room, poked his head under the railing, and peered down at us. In his own way he was announcing, "You may think I'm not the head of his household. But I have other ideas. I may be a few rungs higher in creation than you so-called 'masters.'"

A well-intended decision

One day we learned that a couple from our church had had cairn terriers earlier in their lives. They lived on a small sheep farm just a few miles from us. They said they would love to care for Obie when we were away. We thought it was the perfect solution. Obie would have the love of folks who understood his way of life.

Unfortunately, this part of the story had a tragic ending.

In early 1997, just a year after Obie joined our family and at the point when he was responding well to our training routine, we went to Arizona for a speaking engagement. We assumed Obie would be safe on the farm.

As we drove home from the airport we could scarcely eat up the miles in our longing to see Obie again. Now more than ever we realized how much he had become an important member of our family circle.

As we drove up to the farm home everything seemed eerily quiet. Very slowly the sheep farmer emerged from the front door and came to our car—alone. With trembling voice and shaking hands he said, "Obie's dead. He got out of the house and ran down the road and got hit by a truck."

We were devastated, as were he and his wife. We tried to console them, knowing how deeply hurt they were over the tragedy.

As the story unfolded we learned that the farmer, who often took Obie with him in his pickup on errands to town, had gone to town alone that day. Obie, of course, whined and barked until the farmer's wife let him out the door. She expected him to stay near the house when he saw that the pickup was gone. Instead, he bolted down the long lane and out to the township road. A delivery truck, racing to make its next drop, was speeding down the road. Obie was dead in an instant. The driver didn't bother to stop. A neighbor found Obie and recognized that he was the dog who stayed at the sheep farm.

An unusual good-bye

How do you arrange for disposing respectfully of the body of your little friend in the middle of the winter in a rural area? The sheep farmer explained how he cremated sheep that died in the cold weather. We agreed to return the next day and have the cremation for Obie.

There in the middle of the yard the farmer built a pyre of wood. I carried Obie's lifeless body in a blanket from the barn and placed it on the pyre. We held hands as the flames licked up and consumed his body. The tears flowed freely—ours and those of the farmer and his wife. Obie was off to dog heaven.

Weeping through the snowdrifts

The next day I went to collect Obie's ashes. When I got back to our home I walked through the deep blanket of pure white snow that covered the flower garden. I scattered his remains, weeping as I let the gray ashes settle into the drifts. Next spring's blooms would be nourished by the gift of his body.

I wrote to my family telling them that I felt like a ten-year-old boy who had just lost his best friend.

To our host in Arizona I wrote:

Dear Les,

We're heavy-hearted tonight. We were so eager to see Obie when we got home. As we drove into the farmyard of our friend he came out with the sad news that Obie had been killed that day. It's so quiet around the house. Everywhere we turn there are reminders of that vibrant life that brought so much delight to us.

Today the rabbits are eating undisturbed below the bird feeder.

What a price we pay for love . . .

What I learned from Obie

Play!

After years of preparation for one's career and a lifetime of honing intense work habits, it's not easy to cross the line one day into retirement. Though we long for it for years and dream about all the things we plan to do, it's an abrupt change for most of us. Those ingrained routines tend to follow us into the new arena. The intensity of our daily schedule threatens to become a way of life in these later years. Yes, I had many times of relaxation during my work years, days off and enjoyable vacation times. But now, suddenly, every day is Saturday!

Obie helped me make the transition. He was just plain fun. Difficult as it was for him to learn the good habits of discipline, he could not help but make us laugh again and again in the course of a day.

Even the most serious, workaholic type A personalities need to lighten up now and then, especially in retirement years:

. . . spending a lazy day trolling for walleyes

. . . joining friends for a full week of hunting across South Dakota

. . . creating a new flower bed or vegetable garden

. . . lingering over a morning cup of coffee with our spouse or a good friend

. . . walking two miles instead of one

. . . biking five miles instead of two

. . . rising at five o'clock in summer or seven o'clock in winter just to roam the countryside looking for camera shots when the light is at its best

. . . spending an evening over dinner and extended conversation with friends without worrying about having to go to work early the next morning or catch a flight to some distant city

. . . helping a friend fell a tree and split and stack wood for winter fires

. . . reading a long book in less than a week

. . . visiting lonely folks in the nursing home and not feeling pressure to rush back to the office

. . . singing in the church choir

. . . taking a half-hour nap and not feeling it was a waste of time

. . . enjoying a leisurely eighteen holes of golf rather than racing through nine

Thanks, Obie, for teaching me how to let it all hang out, to go for broke, to love life, to take time to smell the roses, to have fun. I had a tough time teaching you some important lessons. But you taught me the best lesson of all—to play again!

Jonah—a gift from heaven

Sad feelings of loss

After Obie was killed we fell into a deep funk. We didn't want to remove Obie's bed, his toys, his dish, and his collar and leash. But we didn't want to leave them as they were, bringing back memories every time we turned around. I stored them in the big closet in my shop.

Nights were the worst. I didn't sleep well. I'd toss and turn, wondering how to get through the next day without the routine we had come to enjoy with Obie. Everything seemed so grim. How could we recapture some of the spark that Obie brought into our lives?

A thought in the night

As I've learned over a lifetime, it's often in the dark of the night that a ray of hope shines through. Lying awake in the early hours of the morning I wondered: Is it possible that Evelyn and Pete still have those parent dogs? And if so, did they have puppies again this winter? The thought shattered in a moment like a broken mirror. I said to myself: I can't go through this again. And after all the heartache I certainly couldn't expect Corinne to agree to have another dog.

At breakfast the next morning I spooned up my oatmeal without enjoying it in the least. The view out over the lake from our breakfast table, normally a vision to lift one's spirit even on a cloudy winter day, now looked bleak and barren. No, this place just wasn't home anymore without Obie.

I couldn't believe my ears

Was I hearing correctly? Through my gloomy fog and from across the breakfast table I heard a soft voice asking, "I wonder if they bred those dogs again this year?"

Suddenly I was wide awake! Without even asking her to repeat the question I all but catapulted from my chair and rushed to the phone. "Evelyn, this is Herb Chilstrom. We adopted a cairn terrier from you a year ago." I went on to tell her the tragic story of what had happened to Obie. "Is there any chance that you and Pete bred those two cairn terriers again this year?"

"Yes," she said.

I scarcely dared ask, "Are there any puppies left of the litter?"

"Yes," she replied, "We have just one puppy left."

I could hardly believe my ears. "We'll be there in less than an hour."

An unusual, loveable, stinky puppy

When we first laid eyes on this leftover puppy we understood why he had not been chosen. His ears were uncharacteristically long, not the short, spiked ones of the "ideal" cairn terrier. And already it was apparent that this little guy wouldn't remain little for long. He would surely grow to a size larger than the average fifteen to sixteen pounds for this breed.

Evelyn and Pete had all the papers to prove this pup was a genuine, certified, purebred cairn terrier. Any doubt was erased with one look at his quintessential, inquisitive, happy face, the same look we had seen in his older brother.

For us these out-of-the-mainstream traits made no difference whatever. Rearing a show dog was not our aim. This friendly puppy would fit into our family just as he was. Papers were signed and the check was made out without hesitation.

Once more, we were on our way home with a wide-eyed bundle of fur wrapped in a warm blanket in Corinne's arms, just like his older brother Obie a year earlier. Because we had come so quickly, giving Evelyn and Pete little time to bathe and groom him, this little boy smelled to high heaven of urine and all the disinfectants kennel owners use to keep puppies alive and well. Holding her nose, Corinne declared that he would need not one but *two* baths as soon as we reached home.

Is "Jonah" a dog's name?

As we drove the same winding roads through lakes and woods to our home we marveled at how quickly our world of sadness had turned into one of joy and excitement. We also pondered the question of what to name this new "baby" in our family. I suggested that we simply go to the next Minor Prophet in the Old Testament following "Obadiah" and call him "Jonah." "I've never heard of a dog named *Jonah,*" Corinne retorted. But as we drove along she kept looking at him and asking, "Are you little Jonah? Are you little Jonah?" By the time we arrived at our home, yes, Jonah it was.

Hand-me-downs are just fine

Now everything that belonged to Obie was brought out of the big closet in my workshop and handed down to his little brother—collar, leash, bed, blanket, toys, dish—everything was his. He didn't mind at all.

It was a wonderful, heart-warming experience to have a dog in our home again. As we have learned at many other times in life, hope and joy often spring up in surprising ways in the midst of sadness and loss. We felt once again like a complete family.

His own person

Over the next few months we learned that Jonah was not only different in size from his older brother, he was no carbon copy in any way. As in human families, children from the same parents and gene pool differ in sharp and surprising ways in size, personality, and demeanor. Corinne is one of five and I'm one of eight. We see many likenesses with our siblings, but also sharp distinctions in physique, personality, looks, and temperament. Why should it be different in the world of canines?

As I noted in his story, Obie had a brindle hue with an orange-shaded soft undercoat. Jonah was coal black with a grey undercoat, also soft and velvety.

Unlike Obie, Jonah had no need to rip to shreds anything that looked vulnerable. In fact, it was only on the occasion of his first birthday that he seemed to have a need to let loose and express the naughty side of his character. On that festive day he celebrated by tearing apart a shoe of one visitor and mangling the purse of another. It was the only time in his long life that he ever did anything of the kind.

Obie, when he finally realized that he could not be *numero uno,* had tended to bond more closely with me than with Corinne. Jonah made it clear as soon as he arrived that he would give us equal billing. When Corinne placed his soft nighttime blanket next to her side of our bed because there was more space, he ignored it and went to the foot of our bed where he had equal access to both of us.

There would be no need for Jonah, like Obie, to peer down at us from the open staircase. We welcomed him to share the living room furniture with us. He knew, however, that when I wanted my favorite rocker he'd have to move along. Obie probably would have grumbled with a low growl. Jonah never complained, seeming to understand his place in the family hierarchy.

Unlike Obie, Jonah was not a "go fetch" dog. He was a "chase me" dog. When I threw a ball across the lawn he would dash off, pick it up, turn, and stand there with a teasing look on his face as if to say, "You fetch *me.*" When I approached he would take off at breakneck speed, dashing past me first on one side and then the other. Then, stopping with a mischievous look in his eye, he seemed to say, "Old man, you can't possibly catch me."

There was one strong likeness with his older brother. Jonah's afternoon delight on a sunny but frigid winter day was to stretch out on the thick rug in front of the large sliding door that faced the south and catch some rays. Once again I savored my afternoon nap with a friendly companion at my side.

Routine, routine, routine

We agree with those who suggest that dogs need routine. A typical day unfolded like this for us and Jonah:

- out for a pee first thing in the morning
- a small portion of his daily ration (this encouraged him to come back into the house rather than roam)
- morning and afternoon walks, mostly along the same routes
- time for undisturbed naps
- a definite time for his major meal of the day
- opportunities to relieve himself, followed by rewards when he was a puppy
- playtime
- a small snack of Cheerios from my hand followed by a final bedtime visit outdoors

Always—always—there were words of commendation: "Jonah, you're a GOOD BOY."

I wonder how many thousands of times I said those words to him over his long life?

Once we established this routine Jonah adapted to it very nicely—in fact, rigorously! For example, the best time of day for us to give him the main portion of his daily dog food was at three o'clock in the afternoon. If I was in my study and didn't pay attention to the time of day he would come to me promptly at three and tap his nose firmly against my leg. He looked up at me as if to say, "A dog likes to eat on time just as you do." I'd swear he had a clock buried somewhere in his tummy.

Once the routine was set Jonah rarely had an accident in the house. If he did, more often than not we could trace the problem to a break in the routine, improper feeding, or a medical problem. Dogs want to please, even when it comes to peeing and pooping.

Life has its boundaries

To protect him from busy County Highway 4 that ringed part of our lakeshore property, I set up an invisible fence, a buried electrified wire. When Jonah went outdoors by himself he wore a shock collar that sounded a soft bell when he approached the boundary too closely. If he got to the wire the collar gave him a small harmless jolt, just enough to discourage any further investigation. He learned quickly exactly where the line was buried and almost never came near it.

I say "almost never." One day he had a momentary but understandable memory lapse. A cock rooster all decked out in his brilliant red and golden plumage, escaped a nearby pheasant farm. As the proud intruder strutted across the lawn, Jonah caught sight of this alien from the feathered world. This was too tempting. Like a bolt of lightning he took off, chasing the

trespasser across the yard and out the driveway. When he came to the buried wire he jumped a foot off the ground, whirled about and crossed it again, once more feeling the sting of the mysterious charge from under his paws. He never, no matter how tempted, crossed that line again! It may well have saved his life.

When we went for morning and evening walks we crossed that same line in the driveway. At the end of his leash and with no shock collar around his neck, he seemed to understand and never hesitated to cross that line.

Those "ground dog" genes never fail

In every season of the year and every place he goes, a cairn terrier's innate sense of keen hearing and acute smell are on full alert.

When we walked up the country lane in the winter there were at times two or three feet of snow in the ditch. On occasion Jonah would stop and cock his head first to one side and then the other with his ears, like directional antennae, pointing to the ditch. Then, like an eagle diving for a fish, he would leap up in the air and plunge into the deep snow. His head and forepaws were completely buried. All one could see were his hind legs and wagging tail. In a few seconds he would back out of the hole with a vole in his mouth. After carrying it back to the road he would stop, crunch the skull between his strong teeth, and with one gulp swallow the vole headfirst and whole. When the tail disappeared he was ready to move on in search of another delicious morsel.

Who taught Jonah to do this? He had never been to "vole school" or observed another cairn terrier doing this. It was all buried deep in his biological heritage. The world of nature is full of amazing feats like this.

Archenemies

Snakes

Minnesota snakes where we lived were harmless and no threat to Jonah. His first encounter with a garden snake happened one day when he was with me in the potato patch. I had seen this slithering creature before and dubbed it "Big Bertha" because of its unusual girth and length. When Jonah spotted the snake he froze in place. He had never seen anything like this. Standing rigid, turning his head first one way and then another, he took a cautious step toward the snake each time it moved. When it stopped to raise its head and peer ominously at him he emitted a deep but restrained growl. Then, swift as the wolf buried within him, he grasped the snake in its midsection and shook it violently until it fell limp and lifeless to the ground. Then he moved close, stood over it, and uttered another guttural sound, peculiar only to that moment. It was like an expression of ultimate triumph.

On subsequent walks he moved more quickly when he encountered a snake, especially smaller ones. One day as she walked through the meadow with him, absentmindedly enjoying the invigorating smells of the freshly mown hay, Corinne suddenly felt something wet and slimy cross her cheek. It was part of the remains of a snake that Jonah had flung through the air.

Who taught him to do this? Once more, all the genetic imprinting from his cairn ancestors in Scotland, who attacked snakes that emerged from under stone heaps, came mysteriously out of nowhere.

After several years at our Minnesota lake home we began spending winters in Arizona. The north country's harmless garden snakes were one thing. But what about the venomous, sharp-fanged diamondback snakes in the Southwest?

We had built a home in the desert where these natives once claimed prime citizenship. They were not about to relinquish this real estate to anyone without a territorial skirmish.

Friends in the know suggested we take Jonah to "snake school." Each spring as the temperatures rise in the Southwest desert snakes emerge from their winter hibernation. Since it's against the law to kill a snake in Arizona—punishable with a stiff fine—residents call the local fire department to come and "apprehend" snakes and take them out into the more remote desert.

I enrolled Jonah in snake school. On the appointed day we appeared at the pet center where school was in session. A shock collar was placed around Jonah's neck. Against the wall of the building a snake handler sat with a diamondback under control. A long piece of white conduit pipe was placed about six feet in front of the handler and the snake. I was instructed to walk casually around the yard with Jonah and then turn toward the conduit pipe. As soon as the diamondback noticed Jonah, raised its head and began to rattle, Jonah fixated on it. At that precise moment an attendant pressed a button that gave Jonah a shock that made him jump at least a foot off the ground. Jonah retreated quickly. Then I was to try to walk him back toward the snake. He buried his front paws firmly into the ground, refusing to budge even an inch in that direction. He had passed snake school with flying colors.

We had no idea how valuable this lesson would be until we returned to Arizona the next fall. Temperatures were still quite warm and, as we quickly discovered, diamondbacks had not nodded off for the winter. Several days after we arrived I was working at my desk. Corinne and Jonah had gone out into the backyard. Suddenly I heard a blood-curdling scream from Corinne. As I raced through the house—and though I had never heard this sound before—there was that unmistakable clatter like marbles in a tin can. I knew a diamondback was in our yard. I feared the worst.

As I rushed out, the snake had retreated to a low bush. Corinne had no idea where Jonah had gone, thinking the snake may have struck him. She turned about just as I flew out the back door and saw Jonah standing *behind* her. He had done exactly as snake school had conditioned him to do—flee from that sound.

Later I joked that I, too, had learned a valuable lesson that day—hide behind my wife if a snake tries to attack me!

After a call to the fire department the "snake man" appeared and snared the diamondback from the bush. He lifted it with special tongs and deposited it into a tall narrow box with a firm lock at the top. From the fireman I learned a valuable, if very obvious, lesson. I had been feeding birds in the yard. Falling seed had attracted pack rats and geckos, which, in turn, attracted the snake. Lesson learned! We've never seen a snake in the yard in the more than a decade since then. And I hope we never will!

Cows and hay bales

Then there were the cows and hay bales. Jonah was a perfect traveler on our trips to and from Minnesota and Arizona. At times we would permit him to sit on a pad on the passenger's lap in the front seat. From there he could watch the passing cars and enjoy the changing landscape. Cows, however, were among his worst archenemies. When we approached a herd of these bovine beasts he would rise up on all fours and bark like one fending off an invading army of four-legged behemoths.

Then he noticed round bales of hay. These, he surmised, had to be denizens of equal ferocity. At any moment he expected them to come to life, rise up, jump the fence, and attack us.

We soon learned when approaching cattle or hay bales to cover his eyes until the enemies were well out of sight.

Skunks

And then there was the white-striped, odorous enemy. Whenever we came to a spot in the road where a skunk had met its demise, Jonah would pick up the scent long before we did and erupt in barking. These were enemy odors.

One summer day we were relaxing on the deck of our Minnesota lake home as Jonah wandered freely in his shock collar around his prescribed territory. Suddenly we heard what sounded like far-off barking. With no other dogs along our shore, we surmised it was Jonah and that he had somehow eluded the buried wire. I went to investigate. To my dismay he was not far off, but under the storage barn just twenty-five feet from the deck. Then I felt alarm. I could smell the sharp, pungent, unmistakable odor of a skunk! Jonah had cornered one of those smelly varmints under the barn. He was at a place where I could not possibly reach to pull him out. We called and called for him to come out. Then suddenly his barks stopped. We panicked and imagined the worst.

I grabbed a sharp spade from the barn and started digging furiously through rocky ground. When I got down three or four feet I reached in to try to grab him, hoping I would not grab hold of the skunk instead of Jonah! The thought that the skunk might be rabid never even crossed my mind. My only aim was to free Jonah.

We kept calling, "Jonah! Jonah! Come! Come! Over here! Over here!"

Finally, we heard some weak barks. He had begun to come to consciousness again and somehow managed to inch his way over to the hole I had dug. I reached up and pulled him out. He was limp as a rag. Obviously, the skunk had sprayed him repeatedly and directly in the face.

Smell or no smell, Corinne wrapped him in a blanket, just as she had on his first stinky trip home as a puppy. This smell was far worse! We hustled to town and to our vet.

The staff, having encountered this dilemma many times over the years, simply looked at the terrified couple coming in the door and said, long before they caught a whiff of him, "So Jonah got skunked. We'll take care of him."

The next day Jonah ran a high temperature and was very ill. But, thankfully, he survived. I soon enclosed the bottom of the storage barn to make certain our unwanted visitor never got under there again.

In the next days we kept using the tried and true remedies for skunk odor eradication. It worked well, but only to a certain degree. Because cairn terriers have that thick, soft, sponge-like undercoat it took months to completely wash out the skunk odor. If he were outdoors when it rained he would exude faint skunk "perfume" to remind us again of the unpleasant encounter under the storage barn.

Several weeks later when we arrived in Arizona for the winter we left Jonah at the kennel while we were gone for a couple of days. At that time of year it almost never rains in that part of the country. When we came to pick him up a gentle, unexpected rain was falling.

The attendant at the kennel brought out Jonah, accompanied by one of the veterinarians. They had troubled looks on their faces. "I'm very sorry," said the vet. "We let Jonah out for his usual run and it seems he encountered a skunk near the fence. We can't believe this happened. We've never had an incident like this. We've checked him over carefully and he seems unharmed. We've given him a thorough bath and most of the smell is gone."

When we burst into laughter the kennel folks were stunned. They expected a tirade from us and a stern promise that we'd never bring Jonah to this irresponsible place again! When we explained the Minnesota skunk encounter and the rain connection they, much relieved, joined us in a hearty laugh.

Always looking for a "tasty" meal

Like his ancestral "ground dogs" in Scotland, Jonah loved any food he found, dead or alive. After all, these canines had been bred to dig out varmints from under stone cairns, stone fences, and wood piles. If it were a rabbit, for example, and still alive, hunters would shoot it and eat it themselves. But if it were dead it belonged to the dogs, who loved it no matter how long dead, how rancid, or putrid it was. In those ancient times it may have been a major part of their daily diet. Jonah was no exception when it came to salivating over the dead and decaying remains of birds, voles, chipmunks, and you name it.

On one occasion we had just returned to our winter home in Arizona. Sometime over the previous days some kind of creature—probably a pack rat—had died and the remains were in our yard. Baked by the intense heat of the desert, it was everything a cairn terrier could want for a tasty treat. When Jonah's nose led him to this choice morsel he, of course, thought it a gift from heaven. When Corinne saw what he was about to devour, she ran over, grasped him by his collar, and tried to pull him away. Determined not to lose such a delectable dish, Jonah made one grand lunge for the smelly remains and swallowed them whole.

Two days later, on Christmas Eve Day, Jonah became violently ill. Normally a voracious eater, he turned from his dish. We knew a trip to the vet was in order. We told them of Jonah's "meal" in the back yard.

After an x-ray the vet emerged to announce that in his lunge to eat that putrid pile of strange flesh Jonah had also ingested a sizeable stone! It was lodged at the bottom of his stomach, unable to pass further into his intestines and blocking food from passing. It called for immediate surgery.

When Jonah emerged, the vet's assistant presented us with the stone and the bill. I turned to Jonah and said, "Merry Christmas, my little friend!" For a few days he was a bit wan and weary. His sturdy digestive system had easily survived whatever dead creature he ate. But not the stone! After a week or so he was back to his normal, happy self, on the prowl once more for anything spoiled or rotten. We learned that it was better to let him eat whatever he found, no matter how foul. Try to interfere and all of the fierce, aggressive, genetic remnants from his wolf past would emerge. This normally gentle friend might easily mangle one of your fingers.

Good humor, good health, good friends

When Corinne asked one evening how many times in a typical day we laughed at Jonah I could only come up with one reply: "I couldn't count them." And that's how it was. Over and over in the course of a day he brought a smile or a laugh. What a delightful, enjoyable member of our family. If humor is part of overall good, healthful living for us humans, then having a dog like Jonah surely was good medicine.

Whenever the doorbell rang, Jonah was the first to greet our guests. His loud bark sent word through the closed door that this is a happy home. When the door opened guests were greeted with a tail wagging so briskly that one might almost fear it would fall off!

Neighbors who love dogs

In Arizona, Jonah made fast friendships with special neighbors. On the morning walk we passed Richard's home. A retired Montana farmer, Richard loved dogs and has had several of his own. Now it wasn't convenient for him to have one. So each morning Richard rose before the sun and placed a dog biscuit for each of his canine friends at the end of his driveway.

With that kind of motivation, Jonah, even in his older years when we took him part way in the golf car, bounded swiftly the last block to Richard's place for each morning's tasty snack. Richard never failed. At times—and with some slight irreverence—I broke into a song I learned more than seventy years ago in Sunday school, substituting "Richard" for "Jesus":

> Richard never fails,
> Richard never fails;
> Heaven and earth may pass away,
> But Richard never fails.

I'd like to think that Jesus smiled and didn't mind it a bit.

Next door to Richard lived John, another retired Montana farmer. From his breakfast nook each morning he gave a report on Jonah's well-being to his wife Bobbie.

Kathy, another dog-loving and former cairn terrier owner, always carried a few carrots in her pocket when she dropped by, knowing Jonah had a special liking for them.

Butch was Jonah's afternoon pal. A retired Illinois hardware store owner, Butch and his wife Jane loved dogs but also found it inconvenient to have one at this stage in life. Butch converted half of his garage into a workshop. On sunny afternoons the garage door was almost always open. Jonah could see Butch's home as soon as we started off on our afternoon trek. If the door was up, Jonah forgot about peeing and strained at the leash until he heard Butch's unique voice calling, "Jonah! Jonah! How about a cookie?" If Butch were gone for the day Jonah would walk up his driveway and stare intently at his garage door, hoping his strong wishes would make it go up. And on occasion they did!

Good stock

From the start Jonah was blessed with good, vital heath. He must have chosen the right parents. Until he was in his teens, trips to the vet were only for regular maintenance. We gave Jonah all of the attention he needed for good health. The right dog food, fresh water, a vigorous walk morning and evening—all contributed to his ongoing vigor. When gingivitis set in, Corinne made certain his gums and teeth were thoroughly rubbed and brushed each day. The onset of Cushing's disease as he aged—a common canine malady of the kidneys—meant medication to keep it under control.

A companion at death's door

My brother Dave was born in 1933, two years after me. Unfortunately, he sustained some brain damage that left him developmentally challenged for all of his seventy-eight years. Dave loved dogs. His special friend was "Pal," a frisky beagle.

In 2011, after an encounter with prostate cancer, Dave went into hospice care. For many months we visited him, always bringing Jonah with us. Dave took special pleasure in seeing Jonah.

As death drew near we visited more often. One day Dave looked at Jonah and said, "You've been taken good care of." It was his way of affirming our attention to Jonah.

In his final days, and after he had lapsed into unconscious, the nurses lowered Dave's bed closer to the floor so it would be easier to turn him. On the day before he died Jonah leapt up on the bed, stood tall to look into Dave's face and his now comatose body. Then he snuggled against his legs, as though he thought his warm little body would bring some comfort and solace to Dave.

Do dogs understand us humans in mysterious ways as we go through the crises of life? I believe so.

What I learned from Jonah

To live . . .

Because he was our companion for more than seventeen years, Jonah's impact on our lives was substantially greater than that of the first four dogs. From dawn to dusk and through the night he was always there with us and for us. For that reason, the things I learned from him were significantly greater than they were with Duke, Chief, Toto, and Obie.

Here are a few of the qualities Jonah taught me:

Hospitality. I wonder how many thousands of friends and strangers Jonah welcomed to our home over those seventeen years? And how many more that he met on his daily walks and greeted with a vigorous wag of his tail—how many felt a surge of joy when they met him? All were accepted just as they were.

I want to be that hospitable, exuding the same grace and kindness that Jonah showed to us and so many others.

Forgiveness. If I accidently stepped on his paw or reprimanded him for something I learned was not his fault, he forgave me when I stroked him and told him I was sorry. He seemed to harbor no ill will or carry grudges.

I want to be as kind, as forgiving, and as understanding of others as Jonah was of me.

Enthusiasm. Jonah woke up, even in his old age, and began the day with a wag of his tail, anticipating with zest whatever the coming hours held in store.

I want to greet each day with that same hopefulness and joy.

Privacy. Jonah, though genetically a pack dog and in spite of his gregarious nature, wanted others to respect his territory.

I, too, need my privacy, a place where I can be alone with just myself and those I love most.

Acceptance. I can't pretend to know the psyche of a dog. But it seems to me that Jonah was very accepting of his limitations as he grew older. When he realized that something was beyond his capacity, such as leaping up on the sofa, he quietly adjusted to that loss.

I don't want to grow older railing against the increasing limitations I encounter and complaining about every new ache and pain. Instead, I want to give thanks for what has been and adapt to new realities with serenity and hope.

Curiosity. New smells, sights, and sounds, even though muted and muffled by poor vision and hearing loss, still roused Jonah's interest.

I want to continue to be curious and wonder about life and its marvels for as long as I have breath.

Rest. Jonah knew that he needed more rest as he moved deeper and deeper into old age. If he could speak our language he would have said as he curled up, "Oh, how I love my bed."

I want to enjoy my naps and a good night of sleep—to love my bed.

. . . and to die

It has been said that it's good, if possible, for older folks to have a pet. A dog or cat moves in higher speed through the life cycle that we normally traverse at a slower pace. But the message from a dog—from Jonah to us—was clear: We are mortal. Our lives, even at that slower pace, will finally end in death.

Like everyone else, I want to die peacefully, coming to those final days with loved ones near me, grateful for all the good things life has given me, reconciled—so far as possible—with anyone from whom I have been alienated, certain that I am forgiven for the failures and shortcomings that are so evident and, as believers sing in one of our hymns, "fearing the grave as little as my bed."

Will he *make* number 17?

In his last days Jonah helped me to do exactly that. Here's a detailed account of that time in his life.

As we approached the end of 2013 we wondered if Jonah would live to see his seventeenth birthday on New Year's Day. Though his pace was slower and his walks shorter, he seemed to be in no noticeable pain. Periodic laser treatments to relieve his arthritis had helped over his last two years.

He made it! On January 1, 2014, he celebrated his birthday. I guess the seven for one ratio for dogs and humans doesn't necessarily hold for small dogs. If it did he would have turned 119 that day! But even if he was only 95 or 100 in human years, he was still a very old dog.

When it came time for Jonah's regular laser treatment in early February we expected the usual positive results. This time, however, it was clear that there would be no revival of vitality. The treatment did no good. Furthermore, having had such a voracious appetite for all of his life, he was showing disinterest in food. Even Butch's afternoon cookies seemed of little interest to him.

Digging a grave

I knew his time was brief. I began to dig his grave in my vegetable garden in the back yard. It was not an easy endeavor. The top couple of feet were soft soil I had added over the years. But below that the desert was hard clay full of small pebbles. I dug down about two feet and then filled the hole with water to soften the nearly impenetrable clay. The next day I dug another two feet, but it was tough. I covered the hole with a sheet of plywood and loose dirt.

When I finished the task I had some mild feelings of guilt. But they lasted only a moment as I reminded myself that my own grave in Minnesota is prepared as well. The headstone is in place; a marker on the ground has everything engraved on it but my year of death. All that's left to do is dig a small hole and insert my ashes.

Those dreams . . .

Since the death of our son Andrew in the mid-1980s, Corinne and I have had an unexpected journey into the world of dreams. From time to time we've both had remarkable experiences in this mysterious realm of life.

Through our study we've learned that dreams are seldom predictive—telling us things that will happen in the future. Most commonly, dreams aid us in understanding what is going on in our inner selves, serving to help us integrate life's challenges and make responsible decisions.

It was that night, after I dug Jonah's grave, that I had a vivid dream. In the dream Corinne and I were walking happily with Jonah down a country lane. I had the retractable leash in hand. Along the side of the lane was a thick line of evergreen trees, about fifteen to twenty feet high. Suddenly Jonah leapt up on the piney boughs and clambered to the very top. He stood there for what seemed a long time, head and tail erect and looking off reflectively toward "the other side."

Then he started to descend. I feared he might injure himself if he jumped to the ground. I rushed over and got there in time to catch him in my arms.

In the dream we walked on. Then once more he leapt up on the boughs and climbed to the very top, standing straight and tall as he had the first time, looking again to "the other side."

As he descended I ran again to the edge of the trees, expecting to catch him. Instead, he jumped away from me to a place I could not go. I was terrified, thinking he would surely break his legs. But instead, he landed as softly as a bird. He was completely unharmed and looked as he had as a young dog.

As I shared the dream with Corinne over breakfast it seemed there was now no doubt that it was soon time to give Jonah the gift of death.

A quiet, tender farewell

For the next day or two I kept hoping against hope that he might revive. But in my rational being I knew it was time.

That evening before his final trip out to pee I picked up Jonah from his soft bed beside my easy chair in the living room. Friendly as he was, Jonah had never been a lap dog. He would usually squirm after a short time and want to be set back on the carpet. But not this night. He settled deeply into my arms as though he could stay there forever. I stroked his ears, his neck, and his back. Corinne pulled her chair next to us and gave him the same tender attention.

I took him out to the back yard for his last pee of the day. He usually took a brief sniff of the air and turned to go back into the house and off to his bed at the foot of ours. But not this night. He walked to the edge of the patio and stood for a long time peering off into the darkness. I leaned against the house, shedding tears and sensing that he was preparing himself for life's final journey.

Another dream

That night I had the second dream. It seemed ugly and bizarre at first. In the dream I was again holding Jonah in my arms. But this time I looked down and was aghast to see that all four of his paws had been severed! He was not bleeding heavily, just oozing a bit. Then in the dream Corinne brought to me her large chopping knife from the kitchen, the kind with a heavy handle, broad blade, and sharp point. What was I to do with it? I couldn't imagine thrusting it into Jonah's side and killing him.

At that point I awakened from the dream. What could this mean?

It became clear in a short time. Jonah loved to run and run and run. Oh what fun he had when I chased him or when he played with other dogs. Now that was over. Those four little paws would not be running again in this world.

The knife? That, too, seemed clear. This was not a weapon to kill my dog. It was symbolic of the knife that was soon to pierce our grieving hearts.

Final trip to the vet

The next morning I called the animal care center and made an appointment to bring Jonah in at the end of the day.

We walked directly into the small room where he had often been taken for other medical attention. Now it would be the last time. One of the staff persons, a very gentle and kind woman, asked if we were certain we wanted to do this. We both answered with a strong voice: Yes, we were certain.

Soon the veterinarian came into the room. She described what would be done. Then she took Jonah to have a shunt inserted into his front leg. When she returned with him he seemed very calm, possibly slightly sedated, but almost as though he knew what was about to happen.

A peaceful death

Corinne sat in the corner shedding tears. I held Jonah's head in my big hands and leaned close to his ear. In a strong voice, making certain he could hear me, I said for the last of thousands of times, "Jonah, you're a GOOD BOY." I continued to cradle his head in my hands as the doctor administered the fatal dosage through the shunt. It was a quick and painless moment as he took his last breath. His strong heart stopped beating and he went limp. His head fell into my hands.

I thanked the doctor. She wiped tears from her eyes. In that moment I realized in a fresh way what vets go through as they assist families in saying good-bye to their beloved pets.

I wrapped his familiar blue blanket around his body. We avoided the lobby and slipped out the back door.

As we drove home Corinne cradled his lifeless form in her arms, just as she had done seventeen years earlier when he was a new puppy.

While his body was still warm and supple we went to his grave. I slipped him gently into the ground. While Corinne stood by, crying softly, I carefully filled in and patted the soft earth around him. Corinne remembered that *terrier* means "of the earth" and that now for Jonah it was "earth to earth . . ."

The next morning I sent an email note to many who had known and loved Jonah. Among other things, I wrote:

> *Mingled with a brimming ocean of sorrow has been an equally vast reservoir of gratitude.*
>
> *Though he was an atheist, Mark Twain once said, probably with tongue in cheek, that if dogs don't go to heaven, then he didn't want to go either!*
>
> *Well, we're believers, and we can't imagine that the life to come—mysterious as it seems now—will be complete without the companionship of a friend like Jonah.*
>
> *What a price we pay for loving. But would we have it any other way?*
>
> *Corinne sends her love along with mine . . .*
>
> *Herb*

The emptiness

Now it's three months later. We still feel Jonah's presence. Everywhere we turn we see reminders of him.

It happens at the grocery store when we come to the bin of string beans, his favorite veggie, and the Cheerios boxes, his last treat of the day.

When Corinne comes from our mailbox a block away she's often in tears because of all the dogs and their masters she sees out for an afternoon walk.

We smile by the place where he found and devoured a dead, rancid bird not long ago.

At the end of the day when I visit his grave site, I look up into the clear, star-studded desert sky and wonder: Is there more to life than the brief time we spend here in this corner of God's universes? Then I say, "Yes, I believe there is."

Thanks, Jonah, for teaching me how to live—and how to die.

One more dream

Nearly a month after he died I had yet another dream. In the dream Corinne and I were walking along a busy city street. Suddenly I looked down and saw a beautiful cairn terrier at our feet. He was looking up at us with that quintessential cairn terrier face and wagging his tail. But this dog wasn't Jonah. It had a most unusual look to it: a light-grey body and a brindle-hued head.

As I described the dream to Corinne in the morning its meaning seemed clear. Toto was light gray in hue; Obie was brindle. How strange. How beautiful. It was as though Jonah had sent Toto and Obie to cheer our hearts.

Thanks, Jonah . . . you're a GOOD BOY!

Epilogue

The earth and all its creatures

How does one pull together all of the threads of these stories about five dogs I've loved? I found the answer in three places. The first two are from well-known and highly respected German pastors and theologians. The third is from one who has been described as "one of the world's most practical men."

We begin with Helmut Thielicke, whom I cited at the beginning of the book. Thielicke was a popular German scholar and parish minister in the late twentieth century. At times he reflected on creation and the connection between humans and the rest of the natural world. After that elderly gentleman challenged him to "Look a dog in the eye," he could not forget what he had been told to do. Thielicke writes:

> Since that time I have never ceased to ponder at what he said. When I look at a dog and he looks at me those words come back again and again. And though one must guard against sentimentality and reading too much into the situation, I nevertheless cannot shake the feeling that a real dialogue with the creation takes place. And this is the way it sounds: "My little canine friend, you are just one particular part of creation. The two of us—in contrast to innumerable other creatures—have been brought together in a remarkable way and live with one another. If something bad were to happen to you, I would be very upset. And I know that

if something would happen to me, your canine heart would be affected. You notice at once if something is bothering me. And if I am happy, then you make the most comical attempts to show me that you rejoice with me. Sometimes the riddle of creation gazes at me from your eyes so powerfully, so terribly, that you suffer from the burden of not being able to express yourself and to tell me what you know. Of course you can be very expressive with your many bodily motions, with your tail wagging and even with your little paws. But speaking is just out of the question. Sometimes you let me know that I don't understand you. There is a very deep gulf between us that neither of us can cross. And precisely because you are such a unique part of creation, because you have bound your canine destiny to me, a human being, this limitation becomes particularly painful. Our lives are more fully linked than I can say or you can bark."

(From *Being a Christian When the Chips Are Down*, Fortress Press, Philadelphia, 1979.)

And then I came across a brief dog story in a book about the life of Dietrich Bonhoeffer, the German pastor who stood up to Nazism in the 1940s and paid for it with his life. A century ago Bonhoeffer was a young seminary student. He spent a year in Barcelona serving a German-speaking congregation. Here are excerpts from Bonhoeffer's journal.

Today I encountered a completely different case in my pastoral counseling which I'd like to recount to you briefly and, despite its simplicity, really made me think.

At 11 a.m. there was a knock at my door and a 10-year-old boy came into my room with something I had requested from his parents. I noticed that something was amiss with the boy, who was usually cheerfulness personified.

Soon it came out. He broke down in tears, completely beside himself and I could hear only the words, "Herr Wolf ist tot!" (Mr. Wolf is dead!) And then he cried and cried.

But who is Herr Wolf? As it turned out, it was a young German shepherd dog that was sick for eight days and had just died a half-hour ago.

So the boy, inconsolable, sat down on my knee and could hardly regain his composure. He told me how the dog died, how he played with the dog every morning, and how everything is lost now. Each morning the dog came to his bed and awakened him. And now the dog was dead.

What could I say?

He talked to me about it for quite a while. Then suddenly his wrenching crying became very quiet and he said, "But I know he's not dead at all."

"What do you mean?"

"His spirit is now in heaven where he is happy. But tell me now—will I see Herr Wolf again? He's certainly in heaven."

So there I stood and was supposed to answer him, yes or no. If I said, "No, we don't know," that would have meant "No." So I quickly made up my mind and said, "Look, God created human beings and also animals and I'm sure God also loves animals. And

I believe that with God it is such that all who love each other on earth—genuinely love each other—will remain together with God. For to love is part of God. Just how that happens we don't know."

You should have seen the happy face on this boy. He had completely stopped crying. "So then I'll see Herr Wolf again when I am dead. Then we can play together again."

In a word, he was ecstatic. I repeated to him a couple of times that we really don't know how this happens. He, however, knew and knew it quite definitely in his thinking.

This whole affair was as important to the young boy as it is for one of us when something really bad happens. But I am almost surprised, moved with the innocence of the piety that awakens at such a moment in an otherwise completely uninhibited young boy who is thinking of nothing else.

And there I stood, I who was supposed to know the answer, feeling quite small next to him.

I cannot forget the confident expression he had on his face when he left.

(From *Bonhoeffer: Pastor, Martyr, Prophet, Spy: A Righteous Gentile vs. the Third Reich* by Eric Metaxas, Thomas Nelson, 2010.)

More than a half century ago Frank Laubach launched the "Each One Teach One" program that eventually helped an estimated sixty million people around the world to read. What could be more practical and down-to-earth than that?

But Laubach was also an unapologetic person of faith, a mystic who insisted that there is more to life than we can see and touch and measure. One day while viewing a stunning sunset across a lagoon in the Philippine Islands, and with his dog Tip at his side, Laubach penned these lines:

I patted Tip's head as he nestled up under my arm, and told him: "We are two tiny insects in the middle of this terrifying universe. I know a little more than you do, you nice, black dog, but not much more. Compared with the gigantic Being who wheels those awful spheres of fire through the sky, I am as near nothing as you are. I know as little about God as you know about me, perhaps ten thousand times less. And perhaps you are wiser than I, for you are content to be patted on the head and to hunt for fleas, while I am impatient to break loose into the universe. My soul demands immortality as much as it demands God. And it demands freedom from this prison we call the world . . . as much as it demands immortality."

(From: *Letters by a Modern Mystic*, Purposeful Design Publications, 2007.)

"With the earth and all its creatures, . . . we praise you, O God."
(From *Evangelical Lutheran Worship*, page 111, Augsburg Fortress, 2006).